Slow Noticing

This book belongs to...

Name, age,
    date, location, etc.

Slow Noticing

A Journal for
Drawing Your World,
Inside and Out

Mia Nolting

a TarcherPerigee Book

tarcherperigee

An imprint of Penguin Random House LLC
penguinrandomhouse.com

TarcherPerigee with tp colophon is a registered trademark of Penguin Random House LLC.

Most TarcherPerigee books are available at special quantity discounts for bulk purchase for sales promotions, premiums, fund-raising, and educational needs. Special books or book excerpts also can be created to fit specific needs. For details, write: SpecialMarkets@penguinrandomhouse.com.

ISBN: 9780593541197
Proprietary ISBN: 9781101950067

Printed in China

10 9 8 7 6 5 4 3 2 1

Book design by Mia Nolting

For Mikko

Introduction

This book was inspired by my
lifelong habit of keeping a sketchbook.
It contains simple drawing prompts
that ask you to observe your inner
and outer worlds, to see things you
might otherwise miss.
It's a mindfulness journal based on
drawing, or a drawing journal based
on mindfulness. It draws from art
therapy principles, though I'm not an
art therapist.
The goal is not to make a finished
drawing — though that might happen —
but to slow down and record what
you notice.

Drawing windows

What do you see when you look out?

What do you see when you look in?

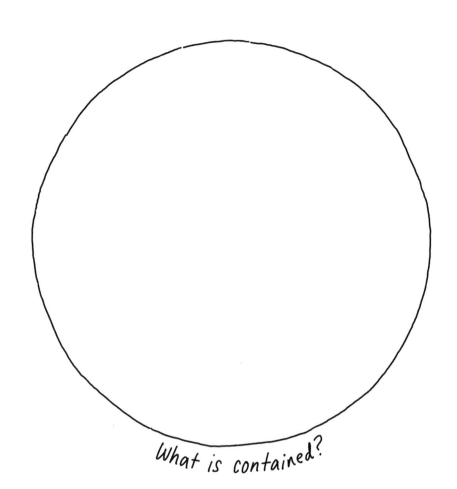

What is contained?

What is not contained?

Trace the path of an ant,
or a spider,
or a small moving insect

Upward-reaching branches

Are they stiff or flexible?
    Are they tangled and thorned?

Are there buds and leaves?
Are they straight or crooked?

Draw something blue
   (night, shadow, subconscious,
      asleep, winter, submerged, quiet)

Draw something yellow
    (light, daytime, energy, summer,
            awake, aware, exposed)

Draw a clock for counting breaths

A clock for counting backwards

A clock for seasons

Constellations

· · · · · · · · · · · · · · · · ·

When do you
connect the dots?

When do points become a shape?

Look into the distance

Draw something in the foreground
    that you can see

Draw something in the foreground
that you can't see

Draw something in the middle ground
that you can see

Draw something in the middle ground
that you can't see

Draw something in the background
that you can see

Draw something in the background
that you can't see

Draw something in the background
of your mind

Drawing the sun

How many suns are in your sky?

Draw five things you notice
        in the physical world

Draw five things you notice
          in your internal world

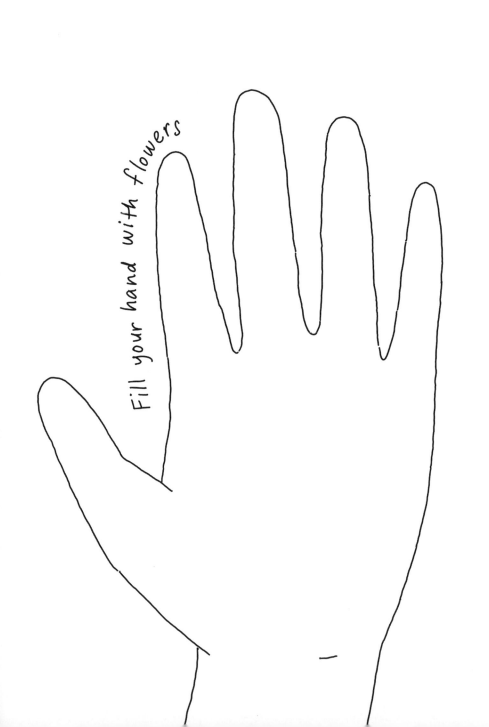

Fill your hand with flowers

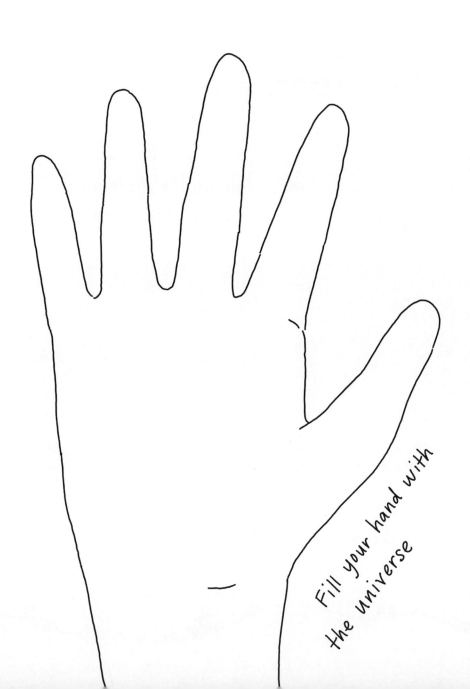

Fill your hand with the universe

Drawing the horizon

Natural or human-made,
  real or imaginary

Find a line in the distance
              and follow it

Find a line in your mind
and follow it

Imagine the face of someone
who isn't here

What does the sound of
their voice look like?

What is behind their eyes?

What does their world look like?

What do you see
   when you look
through their eyes?

Drawing for the seasons

$$\boxed{SPRING}$$

ideas: peonies, rain clouds,
awakening, abundance,
optimism, flourishes, stretching...

SUMMER

ideas: yellow, slowness,
vegetables, wildflowers,
haze, bugs, rivers, fireflies...

ideas: dead things, sunsets,
  cold cheeks, falling leaves,
 wind, twilight...

$$\left(\text{WINTER} \right)$$

ideas: bare trees, cold feet,
sleep, blue, quiet,
softness, wind, night sky...

Different masks for different moods

Draw a body of water

Draw a meadow

What kind of animals live there?
   What colors are the flowers?

                Can you see underground?

Drawing weather patterns

A summer sky

A winter sky

Balancing and calibrating

What is equally weighted?

What is off-balance?

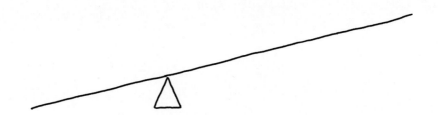

Think of your body, everything
    it can and can't do

Draw its outline and fill the inside
    with colors, patterns, shapes...

A reminder that the breath
is always there:

make a mark for every breath
until the page is full

On transformation—
    draw a caterpillar,
    a cocoon, a butterfly

Draw a collection of special objects

Calming and agitating

Think of a time you were relaxed

What does it look like?

Is it a scene, a color, a pattern,
an object, something else?

Think of something stressful

Hold it in front of you
at a distance

Put it in this bowl:

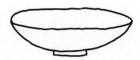

Shine a light into a cave

Is it damp or dry?
 Warm or cool?
What lives there?

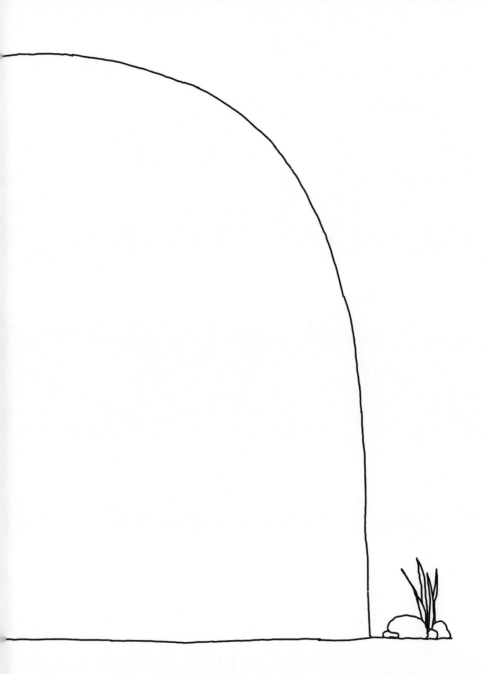

What's on the walls, ceiling, floor?

Symbols of community:
soil layers, orchards,
  forest, jungle, the ocean floor

Something dead and something alive

Threshold:

what's beyond door #1? Door #2?

How many more doors are there?

Draw a recurring dream
(waking or sleeping)

Draw eyes, ears, noses, mouths

Put them
  together, or not

An egg growing something

What's in there?

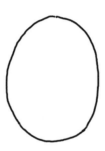

What will it grow into?

A gate, fence, or
    other boundary

Draw the elements
    (or a symbol for them)

                    Earth,

...Air,

...Fire,

...Water

Environments

An open landscape

A thick forest

Draw five things you saw today

A foggy morning
(How do you draw fog?)

Draw a ghost

The ghost of an ancestor

The ghost of something or someone
in your past

Draw the land you occupy from above

Draw a house made out of sticks

A house made out of clouds

A house made out of flower petals

A collection of things
that fit in your hand

Draw an imaginary meal

Drawing faces (no one in particular)

Blades of grass — an infinite field

Draw someone you love
who is in this world

who is no longer in this world

Imagine the land of your ancestors

Is it dense?
Crowded?
Open?
Cold or warm?

Highs and lows as mountain peaks

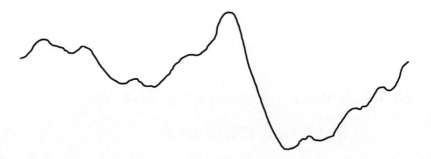

Draw something delicate, shallow,
light, and contained

Draw something deep, rich, broad, and expansive

who lives in this tree?

Drawings for the phases of the moon

(a sliver of something

(half of something

○ almost all of something

○ all of something bright

Draw an imaginary musical score

Peeling back the layers of an onion:

how deep do they go?

Find an object
 —it can be special or ordinary—
    that you can hold in your hand

    Draw its outline

                                        Draw its inside

Draw your hand around it

An imaginary path

What is the
terrain like?

where does it lead?

what do you encounter
along the way?

Draw a self-portrait as a tree...

...as a flower

A portrait of a stranger you saw once
and never saw again

Bus #4

A portrait of someone you've met only
once or twice

Symbols of power and vulnerability

A knife, a rock, a castle...

A flower, an ecosystem, a
small animal...

The edge of a precipice —
    what's on the other side?

A sky full of raindrops, or teardrops

Draw the folds of a raisin,

a pecan, an old face

Draw the rings of a tree...

...the rings of a fingerprint

Ropes and knots and braids

How many parts of yourself
can you identify?

Draw them as shapes

Draw a room

Draw the corner of a room

Draw a river at night,
    the moon reflecting on the rapids
and silhouetted trees and jumping fish

What is the potential
    of these seeds?

What will they become?

Draw and notice the patterns
of a seashell

Draw the sky from a dream

How do you draw a sound?

What goes in the soup pot?
Food or not food,
old feelings,
tomatoes,
stones,
leaves...

Draw a spiderweb

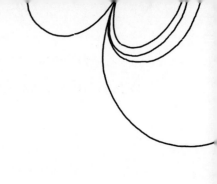

Is anything caught?

Symbols of stability:
mountains, minerals, continents

Symbols of instability:
weather systems, air currents,
wind, seasonal changes

Waves of all sizes:
   ripples, swells, a gentle lapping...

Staircases, real or imaginary

Where do they lead?

Stepping-stones

What are you stepping through?
where do they lead?

Beginnings and endings:
    sunrise and sunset

How are they different?
How are they similar?

Draw a tree at night

A tree in the wind

A tree in winter

A climbing vine

A vast canyon of colored rocks

Watering seeds: what is sprouting?
   Delicate roots,
     tiny blossoms,
       a large tree?

Three ways
to draw flowers

Start from
the outside

Start from
the bottom

Start from
the inside

○ →

A worry basket

What goes in it?

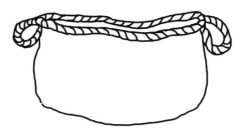

Draw a word, or many words
(Resist the urge to make it
make sense)

A flock of birds
        coming and going,
    resting,
        nesting,
    making sounds

A scene: a crowded sidewalk,
cold sunny weather, busy people
of all ages

A scene: wet concrete after a rain,
    scattered leaves, worms and snails,
        puddles, a barking dog

An imaginary map
   mapping feelings, moods, terrain

physical and emotional destinations

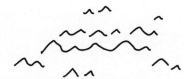

Draw a symbol or image of anticipation

Draw a symbol or image of affection

Draw the current state of your mind:
a train of thought,
connected synapses,
mental images...

Natural objects and
people-made objects

Drawing for the five senses

TOUCH

TASTE

A picture of today

A picture of tomorrow

Draw a fire
A fire pit
A fireplace
A fire escape

Draw mirror images

Notice and draw the veins of a leaf

The veins of your hand

Draw different views of yourself:
   from above,
       from below,

from the side,
etc.

Draw your childhood room...

... and an object that was special
to you as a child

Objects for inside and
        objects for outside

Draw the plant, animal, or person
nearest to where you are right now

Draw something you can't touch
(a planet or star, magma, the
top of a redwood tree...)

Draw something you can't see
(a cell or a virus, some gossip,
a bodily feeling, the wind...)

Draw someone you used to know well
but are no longer in touch with

Draw someone you wish you knew

Something beautiful and something ugly

Draw an echo

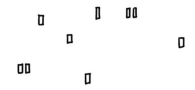

A cityscape full of windows

A skyscape full of stars

A continuous line making nothing in particular

A continuous line drawing of a
nearby object, person, or animal

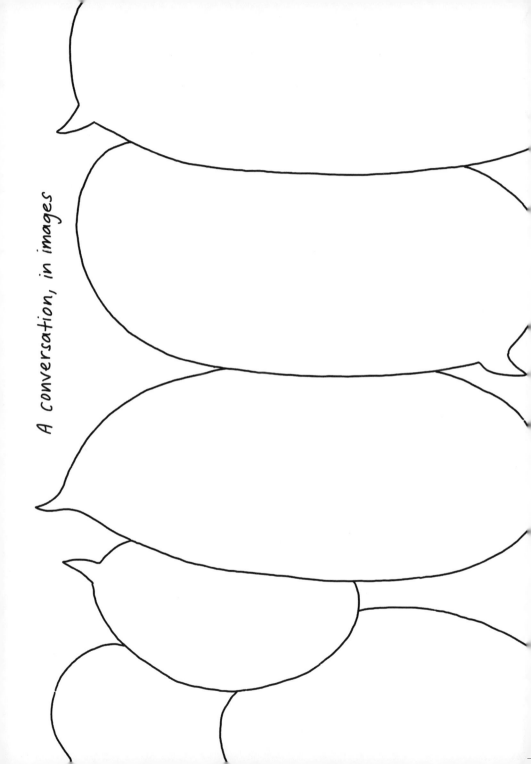

A conversation, in images

Draw a flower with 1,000 petals,
or enough to fill the page

Draw the feeling of a full night of sleep

Draw the feeling of swimming

Self-portrait: how are you seen
        through the eyes of another?

What is on the other side
of the horizon?

↓

_____

Something old and something new

Something lost and
something given away

Morning piece: a ritual, a certain
kind of light, a temperature

A portrait of the moon
through a window

goodnight,
moon

A drawing for the word **yes**

A drawing for the word **no**

A portrait of someone
      who has helped you

A portrait of someone you'd
like to apologize to

Draw a tree in spring, summer...

...fall and winter

A large, deeply rooted tree

A pot of delicate flowers

What lives among
these roots?

Outside during a snowstorm
    (snow weighing down branches,
  a person walking against the wind,
    deep footprints,
        animal tracks...)

Inside during a snowstorm
(a foggy window, a fireplace,
a warm blanket...)

Objects being blown by the wind

Cut a viewfinder to look at the sky

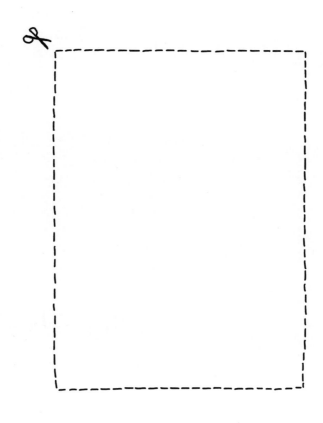

Draw what you see

Draw someone you're grateful for

Something you're proud of

Something simple...

...and something complicated

Pages of infinite possibility

Thank You

Marijke and Oregon Drawing Club

My editor, Marian, at Tarcher Perigee

Vanessa, Rashel, Jelly, Jen, Padraic

Baby watchers: Heather, Linda,
Marijke, Mom,
Fran & Jessica, & Sarah

About the Author

Mia Nolting works at the intersection of writing, illustration, and publishing. Born in Japan and raised in California, she now lives in Portland, Oregon. Her clients include Nike, The New York Times, Whole Foods, and other companies big and small. You can find her on instagram @ mianolting and at mianolting.com.

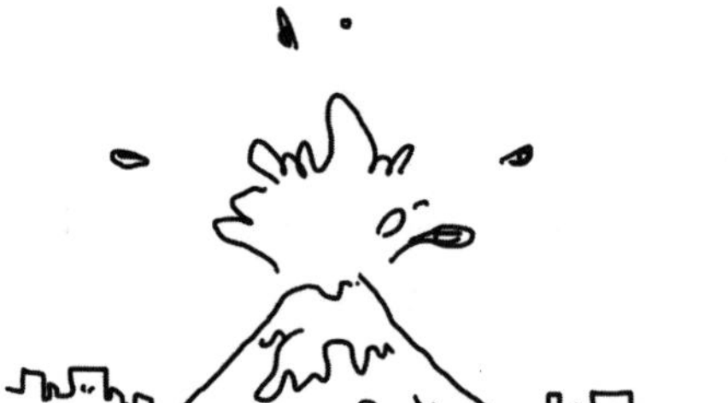